Zoom™ In on

Science Concepts

Air

Andrea Rivera

abdopublishing.com

Published by Abdo Zoom™, PO Box 398166, Minneapolis, Minnesota 55439. Copyright © 2018 by Abdo Consulting Group, Inc. International copyrights reserved in all countries. No part of this book may be reproduced in any form without written permission from the publisher. Abdo Zoom™ is a trademark and logo of Abdo Consulting Group, Inc.

Printed in the United States of America, North Mankato, Minnesota
052017
092017

THIS BOOK CONTAINS
RECYCLED MATERIALS

Cover Photo: iStockphoto
Interior Photos: iStockphoto, 1, 4, 6–7, 9, 10–11, 19, 21; F. Gorgun/iStockphoto, 5; Hung Chung ChihiStockphoto, 7; Shutterstock Images, 8, 15; Rudmer Zwerver/Shutterstock Images, 13; Wave Break Media/Shutterstock Images, 14; Aleksandar Georgiev/iStockphoto, 16–17

Editor: Brienna Rossiter
Series Designer: Madeline Berger
Art Direction: Dorothy Toth

Publisher's Cataloging-in-Publication Data
Names: Rivera, Andrea, author.
Title: Air / by Andrea Rivera.
Description: Minneapolis, MN : Abdo Zoom, 2018. | Series: Science concepts |
    Includes bibliographical references and index.
Identifiers: LCCN 2017931237 | ISBN 9781532120503 (lib. bdg.) |
    ISBN 978164797616 (ebook) | ISBN 978164798170 (Read-to-me ebook)
Subjects: LCSH: Air--Juvenile literature.
Classification: DDC 533/.6--dc23
LC record available at http://lccn.loc.gov/2017931237

Table of Contents

Science 4

Technology. 6

Engineering 10

Art 14

Math 16

Key Stats. 20

Glossary 22

Booklinks 23

Index 24

Science

Air is a mixture of gases. We cannot see air. But it is all around us.

People, plants, and animals need air to live.

Technology

Smoke from factories can make air dirty. This is called pollution.

It can make people sick.

Filters can clean the air.
Air can pass through a filter.

But the filter traps **particles** in the air. This makes the air safe to breathe.

Engineering

Moving air is wind.
Wind **turbines** have long blades.

Wind turns
the blades.

A **generator** is inside the wind turbine. It is connected to the blades. It makes **electricity** when the blades turn.

Art

Flutes and clarinets are wind instruments. They make noise when air passes through them.

An orchestra has many types of instruments. The different sounds combine to make music.

Math

Layers of air surround the Earth. They are known as the **atmosphere**.

The first layer starts at the ground. It goes up about 6 miles (10 km). The air we breathe is in this layer.

The next layer is up higher. It goes up to 31 miles (50 km) into the sky. The other layers are even higher.

THE EARTH'S ATMOSPHERE

EXOSPHERE

THERMOSPHERE

MESOSPHERE

STRATOSPHERE

TROPOSPHERE

- Air is mostly made of nitrogen.
It also has oxygen in it.
Air contains a small amount
of other gases, too.

- Nearly all living things need air
to survive.

- Plants and animals use air in
a process called respiration.
Animals breathe in the air. They
turn oxygen in the air into carbon
dioxide. Plants also take in air.
But they turn carbon dioxide
back to oxygen.

Glossary

atmosphere – the layers of gases that surround the Earth.

electricity – a form of energy that can be carried through wires and used to power things.

generator – a machine used to make electricity.

particle – a tiny or very small bit.

pollution – harmful substances that damage the environment.

turbine – an engine with blades moved by air, steam, or water.

Booklinks

For more information on
air, please visit
abdobooklinks.com

Learn even more with the Abdo Zoom
STEAM database. Check out
abdozoom.com for more information.

Index

animals, 5

atmosphere, 16

blades, 11, 12

Earth, 16

filters, 8, 9

gases, 4

instruments, 14, 15

music, 15

people, 5, 7

plants, 5

pollution, 6

smoke, 6

turbines, 10, 12

wind, 10